NARCI$

MOTHERS.

(It's Not Your Fault).

*The Complete Guide to Understanding and
Healing the Daughters of Narcissistic Mothers,
Healing Covert Emotional Abuse, Removing
Guilt Feelings and Finally Live Free*

DESIRÉE SHANNON

Table of Contents

Introduction

Growing up with a narcissistic mother is a challenge unlike any other. When you are raised by a narcissistic mother, you experience unexplainable pressure from inside the relationship, outside of the relationship, and inside of yourself. This pressure commands you to be a certain person, a person who can shapeshift into any position that your narcissistic mother requires of you, even when she is not present to see it happen.

When I was growing up, the biggest challenges I faced were the fear of the abuse, and the growing realization that absolutely no one believed the abuse I was truly experiencing. At home, I was constantly walking on eggshells, trying not to trigger my mother and her abusive tendencies. Unfortunately, like many other narcissistic abuse sufferers, I had no idea what would trigger her and so I was constantly squirming and conforming to try to fit everchanging rules around who I was supposed to be and how I was supposed to behave. There was never any clarity around what the true expectations were, as they were constantly changing depending on her mood and who she needed me to be to fit her heinous standards on a day to day basis.

Outside of my home, I was still conforming to try and fit her expectations. I was terrified of behaving in a way that would displease her and her finding out, which would make my home life even worse. Or, worse, if I learned to stand up for myself and become my person when I was away from home and I brought that behavior home with me who knows what I would have faced. I was too scared to find out.

No matter how many times I reached out for help, no one seemed to believe how serious the abuse was. Everyone declared that it was just "typical mother and daughter relationship stuff." They believed I was a liar, a drama queen, a bad kid. They had no idea that they, too, had been groomed by my mother. Groomed to see me as a child that should be shunned and shamed, rather than a child who was desperately crying out for help and trying to be protected from the terrifying realities of my home life. She was an expert at keeping me in this position of never-ending abuse.

I swore when I was an adult I would get out of the situation and I would take control of myself. If I could just last a few more years, I'd be free. What I never realized was that by the time I was old enough to escape, I would be too deep in the mess. I wouldn't know how to escape, or where to go, to remove myself from my mother's abuse without losing everything and everyone else that mattered to me. I was trapped, and I had no idea what to do next. It was terrifying, gut-wrenching, and traumatizing.

Many years have passed since this time in my life, and so much has changed. I am no longer exposed to my mother's narcissism because I have learned to step away, create real boundaries, and protect myself. I have learned to heal the traumas I experienced and engage in healthy relationships with other people, and I have rebuilt my life in many ways. I still witness parts of myself that harbor the brokenness that I endured during those years of my life, but as they come up I have the power and the knowledge to heal them and continue moving forward in my life.

To this day, I still have a sense of longing in my heart for a relationship with my mother that could resemble what I truly needed, and what I truly need from her. However, I have come to accept that this is simply not possible and I have learned to fulfill these needs of being nurtured and loved from other areas of my life, including from within myself. While

I don't think this feeling will ever fully go away, it no longer keeps me up at night feeling trapped in the worst possible version of a mental prison. I have learned to stand on my own two feet, and I am forever grateful for that.

In my healing journey, I have come to understand that narcissistic mothers are not nearly as uncommon as I once thought they were. Many daughters grow up with narcissistic mothers who expose them to similar abuse as I was exposed to as a child. I now realize that in healing, I also need to share my message and my knowledge to help other women heal from their traumatic mother-daughter relationships.

Take my story, and my advice, as being evidence that you can heal. There is hope after narcissistic abuse, and there is a way for you to feel whole and nourished in your life. That aching, longing, writhing feeling you hold onto the inside of you in every way is not a life sentence, and you are not doomed to experiencing abuse in all areas of your life for the rest of your life. You are more powerful than you know, and accessing your inner power starts with acknowledging the reality of your mother's wound and honoring and healing the pain that exists within it.

As you read through this book, I strongly encourage you to take your time and to surround yourself with loving people who can help you. Choose at least one or two people who believe you, and who can hold space for you as you uncover, face, and heal the traumas that you carry inside. Having this support will prove to be immensely powerful in helping you to stay grounded and focused during your healing experience. As well, take this at your own pace. There is no race in healing. This is your healing experience, and you need to do it in your way if it is truly going to support you with experiencing life changes.

Don't forget to leave a short review of this book on Amazon if you enjoy it, I'd love to hear your opinion!

If you are ready, let's begin.

Part One:

What Is

Narcissism?

Chapter 1

DEFINING NARCISSISTIC PERSONALITY DISORDER

One of the best tools I have used to heal myself and my traumas due to my relationship with my narcissistic mother is education. Educating yourself on everything that you can around narcissistic personality disorder, how it plays out in mother-daughter relationships, and how it has directly affected you as well as your symptoms can support you understand what you are experiencing. With this increased understanding, you can begin to identify where you are experiencing symptoms of this dysfunctional relationship in your life, why, and what can be done to help you heal them.

Let's start at the beginning of the equation: your mother. Your mother has likely been narcissistic since well before you were born, meaning you have been exposed to her narcissistic behaviors all your life. You have probably never known anything different. For this reason, we can conclude that the beginning of your problems around this starts with your mother and her disorder.

What Does Narcissistic Personality Disorder Look Like?

Narcissistic personality disorder itself is a mental condition that gives people an inflated sense of self-importance, dysfunctional relationships, an excessive deep-seated need for attention and admiration, and a complete lack of empathy for other people. Even though this is what they are experiencing, their symptoms can look somewhat different on the outside. This is because narcissists develop what are known as "masks" which are a sort of alter-ego that they hide behind to cover up the fact that there is something wrong with the way they behave. They use these masks to fake empathy, create false relationships with people in a way that does not reflect who they are truly are, and to create a genuine belief within themselves and others that there is nothing wrong with them.

The symptoms you are likely to see in a narcissist include an incredibly exaggerated sense of self-importance which often manifests as them behaving as if they are better than everyone else, and lying to make others believe it is true, too. They also have a sense of entitlement and feel as though they should get everything they want, including unlimited amounts of admiration for what they do. They often want to be recognized as superior to others, even without a reason to be recognized as so, and they fantasize about having unlimited success, power, brilliance, and beauty. A narcissist will also obsess over having the perfect everything in life, including the perfect house, the perfect mate, the perfect friends, and the perfect anything else. In their opinion, perfect things match their perfection, adding to their level of superiority over everyone else.

Narcissists can often be seen monopolizing conversations while also belittling or looking down on people who they believe to be inferior to themselves. They will often have a few people they seem to belittle the most, which are generally the ones who end up being their long-term victims for narcissistic abuse in many ways. However, they will belittle just about anyone as long as they can get away with it without tarnishing their perfect image, even though this image is all in their minds. Their inflated sense of self-importance also leads to them believing that they should get anything they want in life, no questions asked. They genuinely believe that people should just give in to what they desire without any struggles or difficulties in making it happen. Because of this, they will frequently take advantage of other people and treat them badly, with seemingly no understanding as to what they are doing and no compassion or empathy for the outcome of their actions.

Despite what it looks like on the outside, narcissists are highly envious of others which is largely the reason behind their constant bragging and self-inflating behaviors. They believe that when they act in these exaggerated ways that others envy them and wish to be them, which gives them an even larger feeling of self-importance.

The combination of all of their symptoms leads to narcissists being arrogant, haughty, conceited, pretentious and boastful. They are often the ones that appear confident to a fault, often to the point where people do not even believe that they are as confident as they truly claim to be. However, this is not always the case. Many narcissists have mastered experiencing an inflated sense of self-importance without coming across as overly confident, arrogant, or pretentious because they have come to realize that this does not serve their bigger mission. If they have come to realize that this behavior does not afford them the admiration and affection they desire, they will often tone down their behavior to increase the admiration and affection they receive. They can expertly shapeshift to fit any situation they need to, to get what they desire from that situation.

In private settings, narcissists are extremely unpredictable. They have severe interpersonal problems and can easily feel as though they have been wronged by others, leading to them reacting with rage. They may also react with rage or impatience if they feel that they are not receiving adequate special treatment from those around them. Narcissists struggle to deal with stress, regulate their emotions and behavior, and adapt to change. They can often become moody and depressed because they see their shortcomings and it makes them feel worse about themselves, which triggers their deep-seated insecurities, shame, and humiliation that they feel. These deep-seated feelings often come from realizing that they are not the same as others and fighting desperately to fit in, yet not knowing how to do so in a way that is not abusive and damaging to those around them. Even so, they will never admit this to anyone, under any circumstances.

What Causes Narcissistic Personality

Disorder?

The true cause or causes of narcissistic personality disorder are not known. Doctors cannot pinpoint any one thing that causes narcissism in people, so there is no way of knowing what may have caused your mother's condition. With that being said, some psychologists and doctors have come to suspect that a series of three things can contribute to narcissistic personality disorder. These three things include the environment, genetics, and neurobiology. There is no guarantee that these are the reasons, but they are suspected to at least contribute to the development of narcissistic personality disorder.

The environment is believed to affect the development of narcissism when an individual is raised by a parent who either excessively adores or excessively criticizes the child. If your mother was raised by parents who were poorly attuned to your mother's needs and who overly babied her or who excessively criticized her, this may have contributed to her narcissism. She may have also directly inherited it from her parents. As well, there may be an alteration in your mothers' brain that creates a disconnect between behaviors and thoughts, which contributes to the development of narcissistic personality disorder.

Are There Any Cures for Narcissistic Personality Disorder?

Because there are no known causes for narcissism, there is no known cure for it, either. Furthermore, most people who have narcissistic personality disorder will not acknowledge that they have it and so they will never take action to attempt to treat their narcissism. As a result, they end up having it for life and there are unlikely to be any improvements in their symptoms. Despite what you may think, if a person with narcissism does not want to admit that they have this disorder, which they are highly unlikely to, there is nothing you can do to make them see the truth. They will never truly see, accept, or own their behaviors and actions because this is in direct contradiction to what they are attempting to achieve.

If a narcissist does agree to get treatment, the best thing they can do is attend therapy. Independent therapy and family therapy are both methods that can be used to help a person with narcissism understand how they are affecting those around them, and how their behaviors can be changed and improved. In some cases, changes may occur and the individual may become easier to be around.

Chapter 2

THE NARCISSISTIC MOTHER

The way narcissism manifests in mothers specifically is unique, as children see their parents in a way that no one else does. Even a healthy relationship between a child and a parent is likely to be experienced in a way that is unique to them, not anyone else. Mothers tend to be more comfortable around their children, meaning that they can open up and express their true selves better around their children. For mothers who do not have narcissism, this is generally shown in a gentler and softer, nurturing manner. For those mothers who do have narcissism, however, this is generally a relationship where the narcissism will play out in a far more offensive and overwhelming manner than it would in any other relationship. In other words, narcissistic mothers tend to abuse their children, especially their daughters, more than anyone else.

Understanding how narcissism manifests in mothers is the best way to identify where your mother is abnormal compared to other mothers, and how these abnormalities are linked to her narcissistic personality disorder.

A Mother That is Threatened by Her Child

Narcissistic mothers often experience the feeling of being threatened by their children in the sense that they worry that their children are likely to take attention and admiration away from themselves. When narcissistic mothers notice their children are getting attention around any given subject, such as excelling in school, they will often begin to feel threatened and will attempt to minimize the value of the child's achievements.

A big way they do this is through how they talk to others, using sayings like:

- "*Finally,* you're good at something for once!"
- "It's about time you bring home an award for something."
- "Wait, you mean you did something good? Wow."

Speaking in a way that makes it seem like the child is otherwise terrible is a way that a narcissistic mother can control the amount of attention the child receives. They may receive attention around this one thing, but through her words, she tarnishes the child's reputation and therefore prevents the child from receiving further accolades anywhere else in their lives. This way, she can earn those accolades for herself and gain all of the excessive attention and admiration she needs from others.

An Effort at Self-Fulfillment Through You

Another big way that narcissistic mothers can be identified through their symptoms is through attempting to inflate their sense of self through you. My mother often did this by attempting to take credit for every positive thing I did in my life, making it appear as though she was the only reason, I had anything good going for myself. She would frequently use this as a way to take the attention away from me and put it on herself, even when it did not make reasonable sense for her to do so.

For example, as a child, I used to get excellent grades in school and every time my report card came home with several A's on it my mom would make dinner complete with all of my favorite things, which happened to be her favorites, too. She would go on to say how this was going to be an evening to celebrate me and my achievements, making me feel like maybe I had finally received her praise. Maybe she was finally proud of me. Every time, however, she would spend the entire dinner – my special dinner – talking about how she was responsible for my success. She would say things like how I would not be here without her, and how this proves that she is such a great mother, even going so far as to point out that I was cruel and mean for claiming otherwise when I called her out on her abuse to a family member one time

To add insult to injury, any time I would ask my mother for help with my homework she would either downright refuse or spend the entire time yelling at me for not being good enough, although it was her who was misunderstanding the assignments. In other words: I earned those A's in spite of her, not because of her. Over time I grew so resentful that I stopped caring about my grades at all because it was painful to have something, I was proud of ripped away and used as a tool against me constantly.

Narcissistic mothers frequently live through their children or use their children as a way to further inflate their sense of self. They generally do this because they know that at young ages children are not able to identify what is going on, and therefore they cannot stop the abuse from happening. By the time they are old enough to speak up, the mother has either made them too afraid to try or has already groomed everyone else to believe that the child is a problematic liar so that no one believes the child. In the end, the child is forced to live in a mental prison that is shaped and manned by their parent, which is a form of torture that no child should ever have to experience.

The Development of a Superficial Image

Another way that you can spot a narcissistic mother is in how they portray themselves to people outside of your family, or even outside of your relationship with her. Yes, narcissistic mothers will frequently wear several different masks even within one household, for example: abusing her child in private and pretending nothing ever happened when the child's father is around.

The development of a superficial image that portrays your mother as someone who never does anything wrong is a strategy that she uses to protect herself from her consequences. She does this to groom others into believing her, and not her child, which means that she can protect her primary source of being able to fulfill her cruel and unusual needs. This way, when she openly belittles and bullies her child the people around her believe it is warranted and the child has no hopes of escaping the experience.

Chapter 3

A NARCISSISTIC MOTHER'S DAUGHTER

Symptoms in a narcissistic mother-daughter relationship are not exclusive to the mother. Daughters who have been raised by narcissistic mothers are also subjected to experiencing many of their painful symptoms that can lead to many problems in the future. You need to take the time to look at yourself as a part of the equation to see what symptoms you are experiencing, and to understand how they may be influencing you to experience more problems or abuse in your adult life.

Looking at your symptoms can be painful because you are going to have to face everything that you now experience and understand that this was all due to your mother. You might feel an intense amount of rage, sadness, pain, grief, guilt, or other emotions relating to these discoveries, so I strongly encourage you to make sure you can speak to someone you trust after reading this chapter. Being prepared to receive support as soon as you need it when difficult emotions or memories come up can be helpful in your recovery from this abuse.

You May Be Chronically Ashamed of Yourself

Daughters of narcissistic mothers are known for experiencing chronic shame in their lives, particularly around everything relating to who they are and what they do. It may feel like there is no limit to the shame that you experience, and that you tend to experience it in many different ways.

The shame that you experience now stems from always being made to feel inadequate as a child. Narcissistic mothers tend to be especially threatened by their daughters, which means that the level of abuse that you have experienced in terms of being put down and bullied is likely enormous. There is a good chance that your entire childhood was spent with you being told the many reasons as to why you were a bad person, and why you were not good enough. You were probably told that you were not deserving, not pretty, not smart, not worthy, and many other untrue things that were said to get you to stop bringing attention to yourself.

By making you feel horrible about yourself, your mother could feel confident that you would stay quiet and hidden all on your own so that she did not have to attempt to do it for you. She also would not have to take responsibility for dragging your name through the mud or spreading bad rumors about you, which is a common narcissistic behavior known as "smearing." In some ways, your mom may have even used your low self-esteem to increase her sense of importance, such as by bragging about how she had to stand up for you or try to build you up in certain situations because you lack self-esteem. Of course, she would never mention that your lack of self-esteem came from her in the first place because this would take away from her perfect image.

As an adult, you may now experience chronic shame around everything in your life even when you know it is not needed. You might hold yourself to unreasonably high standards, feel guilty about things that are normal human experiences, and attempt to behave like a superhuman because you have been told that you are not good enough. These behaviors are likely both an effort to be seen as a good person and an effort to avoid being abused any further because in your childhood you would be abused if you did not fight to achieve these unreasonable standards. This shame is extremely toxic, painful, and life-altering, which is why we are going to spend so much time addressing and healing it in part 2 of this book.

Childhood Abuse May Lead to Adulthood Abuse or Toxic Relationship Patterns

Any form of childhood abuse can lead to children growing up and entering abusive and toxic relationships, and a child abused by a narcissist is no different. It is possible that as an adult you are now finding yourself in many toxic relationships, or relationships that are even downright abusive. You might feel like you have some sort of hidden "signal" that somehow calls in people who will take advantage of you, bully you, or abuse you through narcissism in your adult life. Many daughters of narcissistic mothers feel as though they cannot get away from narcissism, even though they were sure that leaving their childhood homes would suffice.

The reason why you may be experiencing toxic or abusive relationships now in adulthood is that you have never been taught boundaries or important self-care steps in life. Being raised by someone who commanded you to live your entire life based on her needs and desires has resulted in you not knowing how to fully stand up for yourself and take care of yourself in relationships now. This may be painful to admit, but, indeed, it is likely the reason why this is happening. If you notice that you seem to be surrounded by people who abuse you or take advantage of you and you cannot seem to understand why this happens, there is a good chance that it is a product of your groomed behaviors.

You May Reflect Some of Your Mother's Symptoms

As a daughter of a narcissist, this can be one of the more scary symptoms that you may face. It is one thing to feel unsafe with others, but to feel unsafe within yourself and to recognize yourself behaving in ways that you do not like can be downright terrifying. There is a chance that now as an adult you reflect some of your mother's symptoms, and this can lead to an intense fear that you are going to become abusive toward someone you love just like she did. You may not understand why these behaviors or exist or have any clarity around how far they will develop too, leaving you feeling powerless and as though it may be inevitable for you to follow in her damaging footsteps.

Believe it or not, even though many people do not like to talk about this point, it is quite common in those who survive narcissistic abuse from a parent specifically. The reason for this symptom is that as a child you are supposed to be raised by a nurturing guardian who can guide you to learn how to navigate various parts of life. Ideally, a healthy guardian should have taught you how to deal with difficult emotions, conflict, expectations, self-esteem, insecurities, and other natural parts of life. Unfortunately, you were raised by a mom who did not know how and who regularly modeled extremely poor examples of how an individual should deal with these things. As an adult, you reflecting this behavior is unlikely to be you displaying true narcissism and more likely to be you displaying poor coping methods in life. With proper healing and efforts, you should be able to identify new ways for you to cope with things in life, enabling you to move beyond the patterns of repeating your mothers' behavior due to not knowing a better way.

There May Be the Feeling of a Deep Void in Your Life

One of the most painful things that I have experienced as a daughter of a narcissist, even to this day, is that void that you feel in yourself and your life around your mother. As an adult, you may now find yourself longing for a positive relationship with your mother, possibly to the point where you keep attempting to have a better relationship with her only to find yourself trapped in the cycle again and again.

This is a common experience for daughters of narcissistic mothers and I want to tell you right now that this is not a poor reflection of you, instead, it is a painful reflection of your reality.

Even when you heal yourself from your mother's abuse, you are likely to find yourself in moments where you wish you had a healthy, supportive mother to rely on. You might even recall the times your mother showed you her charming mask, leading you to feel like maybe you can call her for support on just this one thing, hoping that she will offer that type of charm and support once again. It can be painful when you realize that your mother is unavailable to offer you the support and the love that you need, and even more painful when you realize that she has no idea why you feel so disconnected and alone in the world due to her treatment. This is a natural part of the recovery and healing process, and in time it does become a lot easier to navigate. While the pain itself is always there, you will find that you become much stronger in healing that pain and coping with it when it rears its head. This way, you do not put yourself in a game of yo-yo with trying to get your mother to be the woman you need her to be when she truly can't be.

Chapter 4

THE FUTURE OF
YOUR RELATIONSHIP

The future of what your relationship will look like with your mother is ultimately going to depend on you and what you think will be the best for your situation. With that being said, I strongly advise taking a lengthy break from talking to your mom while you heal yourself from her abuse and then ease yourself back into any sort of relationship you might share if this is the path you choose. Attempting to heal from your mom's abuse while keeping yourself trapped in the cycle by maintaining a fairly close relationship, or at least a consistent relationship, during the healing cycle can disrupt your results. You might find yourself constantly getting dragged back in despite how much effort you put into healing, which can leave you feeling extremely poorly about yourself.

With narcissistic mothers there are generally three ways that the relationship can go: you can break away entirely, you can have a small relationship, or you can have a consistent relationship with strong boundaries. What you choose will depend on your chosen coping methods and the level of relationship that you can personally handle without feeling impacted by her abuse. This means that after your break you should slowly build your relationship back up and not exceed what feels right for you, to ensure you do not get sucked into old behaviors that could lead to a complete relapse in your relationship.

What to Do If Your Relationship Must End Completely

The idea that your relationship with your mother might need to end completely can be incredibly painful, especially if you have spent a large portion of your life hoping it would get better. Until this point in your life, you may have been under the influence of the belief that you could somehow contort yourself to make things better and that this would lead to your mom like you more and your relationship is fixed. Unfortunately, this is not real and there is no true hope of your relationship ever being the one that you want it to be, as hard as that is to admit. Believe me, it took me a long time and many relapses in my relationship with my mother to realize that she was never going to be the nurturing, supportive, loving mother that I wanted and needed.

If you find yourself in a position where your relationship must end completely, it might be since your mother's abuse is extreme, possibly on the brink of violent, or causing severe toxicity and trauma in your life. Your mother may be abusive to the point where you cannot have even one conversation with her without her creating a web of abuse, which leads to you feeling like you need to end the relationship completely. In this case, what you need to do is completely cut all ties and keep those ties cut. If you find yourself in a situation where the severity of the narcissism is so advanced that you must cut ties, you must remember why the situation got this advanced. When you find yourself wanting to relapse into a relationship with your mother, you must remember the reason why you no longer have a relationship with her in the first place. If you go back and forth in relationships that are this damaging it can be even more damaging as you begin to experience the trauma from your mother, as well as the trauma from yourself each time you "allow" yourself to get sucked in. This can become a huge point of guilt, and it can make healing even harder, so it is strongly advised that if you make this decision you stick to it.

What to Do If You Need to Minimize Your Relationship

In some situations, you may not need to, or maybe you can't, completely end your relationship with your mother. In this case, it is ideal that you minimize your relationship with her. Minimizing your relationship can look however you want it to look, but ultimately it requires you to avoid seeing or talking to your mother consistently. You might find yourself only talking to her when it's the holidays and you are together at a family gathering, or possibly up to once or twice a month. The frequency of this relationship ultimately depends on you and what you genuinely feel that you can handle with your mother.

This is the area where I fall with my mother. The rest of my family is quite close and I want to make sure that I maintain a relationship with them, which inevitably means that I need to be around my mother from time to time. Aside from these visits, however, I do not contact my mother because it does not feel right for me to do so. I feel stronger when I experience life on my own than I do when I attempt to celebrate with or confide in my mother only to be met with emotional unavailability and abuse. For that reason, this is my best coping method. Even with the minimal amounts of time we see and talk to each other, it still takes immense strength for me to stand strong in my coping methods and refrain from getting sucked into my mother's drama and abuse.

What to Do If You Need to Stay Consistent in Your Relationship

Some daughters will continue to have a fairly consistent relationship with their mother, even after they heal from narcissism. This is often very uncommon, however, as it can be extremely challenging to remain truly removed from the dysfunction when you are still regularly being exposed to your mother and all of her symptoms. The daughters who do find themselves capable of consistently communicating with their mothers and maintaining high-frequency relationships require massive amounts of strength to be able to uphold their boundaries and stay strong. It is incredibly challenging to break the dynamic between the mother and daughter in this scenario because the mother already has it so ingrained in her, and it is all the daughter has known since birth. In these relationships, the mother often knows exactly what to say to push the buttons of her daughter to force her back into the abuse cycle.

Due to the complexity of narcissism and the tact and calculated abuse they dish out, it is important to realize that the likelihood of you being able to maintain a consistent relationship with your mother and heal from her abuse is highly unlikely. If you do attempt to retain this type of relationship, there is a good chance that you are doing so because of her grooming and conditioning to force you to believe that it is required and that you are somehow a bad person if you don't. It may even be due to her smearing you and abusing you if you do try to stand up for yourself and get away from the abuse.

Make sure that if you are going to try this that you strongly consider why you are doing it and that if you must, you constantly work on increasing your strength and boundaries and upholding them in your relationship. You can never let your guard down here, or your mother will see the opportunity and attempt to take advantage of it. No matter how far you may get with protecting yourself, your mother will always be attempting to abuse you throughout your entire life. She will likely even go so far as to use compliance as a way to show you that the relationship can be "all better" to reel you in, just to start the dynamic all over again. You must always be cautious and in control of this relationship, no matter what. For that reason, it is likely going to be far too draining for you to uphold and it is not a good idea to aim for this type of relationship.

Chapter 5

BELIEFS YOU HAVE
DEVELOPED

The final element of the entire puzzle of your trauma from your mother's narcissism is your belief system. Your belief system is a system of beliefs that you cultivate throughout your childhood, adolescent, and adult life that help dictate how you think, perceive and feel about the world around you. Psychologists say that until you are 7 years old, the beliefs you have are entirely taken on by your parents and other authority influences in your life and that any beliefs you create in this time of your life lay the foundation for the rest of your experience. While you can change beliefs from this period of your life, you can only do so if you can become aware of those beliefs and do the healing work on them.

Identifying your beliefs now is going to help you

have a strong understanding of the entire image of your experiences with your mother, which will enable you to create the strongest healing plan for yourself. The concept behind this is that the more you are aware of your wounds and why they exist, the more you can heal.

Some of the beliefs that you may have picked up from your childhood include ones like you live only to serve others, and you are not good enough or worthy enough of having a good life. There are many other beliefs that you may have picked up, however, that you are going to need to consider so that you can start healing them. Some of them you might find in this chapter, others you might find as you go through your healing journey and become aware of them through the healing practices you will engage in. There is no right or wrong answer as to what beliefs could have formed from this relationship, so take note of all of them. Use this chapter, however, to start laying the foundation of this understanding.

You Live Only to Serve Others

This is one of the biggest beliefs that daughters of narcissistic mothers develop in their lives. The belief that you only live to serve others can manifest as people-pleasing behaviors and codependency, so if you find yourself behaving in either of these patterns it may be due to an underlying belief that you are only here to serve others. This belief is formed when your mother makes it clear to you from a young age that you must please her and serve her every need for her to like you. Otherwise, she is likely to withhold affection, respect, and love from you throughout your life. As you see this playing out, you develop a deep-seated belief that your role in the world is to serve others and that serving yourself in any way, including through taking basic care of yourself, is selfish and bad. Alongside this belief, you might also find yourself attempting to shrink yourself and minimize the amount of space you take up in a room both physically and in terms of your actual presence to avoid being seen. In your belief system, being seen may feel like you are taking attention away from someone else which you have been taught is a bad thing due to your mother's need for excessive amounts of admiration and attention.

You Cannot Do Anything Right

As you grow up with a narcissistic mother there is always volatility to the situation because you can never tell what is going to set her off or cause her to punish you in some way, either through withholding nurturing or through rage. Through her behavior, you begin to realize that she could blow up at anything you do, which can lead to you feeling like you can never do anything right. It is likely that through her words she also reinforces the belief that you are bad at everything, making you truly believe that you are incapable.

Your Perception of Reality is Not True

A big and often dangerous belief system that daughters of narcissistic mothers grow up with is that their perception of reality is not true. This mistrust in their perception of reality leads to the belief that they are incapable of recalling events as they happened, and it is caused by narcissistic mothers lying to others and to their daughters to cover up their abuse. This chronic lying and twisting of events can make it feel like you are incapable of remembering anything factually, which leaves you believing that you have to rely on others to recount facts for you because you are incapable. This can be particularly dangerous as it can completely distort your sense of reality and leave you trusting in the wrong people to provide you with a true sense of reality. The truth of the matter is, the only positive way to work through this belief system is to reinforce your trust in yourself and learn to believe in your perception of reality. It is never a good or safe idea to place this trust and task outside of yourself as it will leave you vulnerable to abuse while also keeping your sense of self-esteem, self-confidence, and self-trust low.

Part Two:

Healing and Freeing Yourself

Chapter 6

PREPARE YOURSELF FOR THE EXPERIENCE

N ow that you are fully aware of what the entire spectrum of your abuse dynamic looks like, or at least aware of the basic foundation of it all, it is time for you to begin the process of healing from the abuse that you have endured. Before you can dive into the healing process, I strongly advise that you prepare yourself for what the healing process is going to be like.

For many individuals healing from narcissistic abuse and trauma, knowing what to expect can make navigating the healing process a lot easier. Without the ability to navigate it clearly, you can find yourself feeling almost a sense of shock for what you are facing which can leave you wanting to return to the abusive situation to regain comfort. It may sound silly from the outside, but from the perspective of someone who has been abused, it makes sense that they would desperately cling to any sensation of comfort, even if that comfort is coming from a toxic place. When you live an incredibly uncomfortable life, you will take whatever scraps you can get to feel better and losing touch with those can feel vulnerable and scary, especially when you know how much danger you could be exposed to in doing so.

When I was recovering from my narcissistic mother's abuse, I went back and forth a few times before finally escaping the dynamic. It took me some time to completely accept what I was going through and the pain that I was experiencing and to be able to endure the discomfort I felt during the transition from being the codependent daughter of a narcissist to being an independent adult. Preparing yourself may help you make the move more effectively and transition in a way that is less traumatic and overwhelming to you as you seek to live a healthier life for yourself.

There are multiple steps you can take to help you prepare to move out of the traumatic dynamic and into one that is going to be more stable and healthy for you. You must complete all of them before you start making any bigger moves, as this will give you something stable to transition with, which will make it easier for you to completely escape from the dynamic.

Understand the Cycle of Narcissism

To truly understand what you are about to go through when you break yourself out of the cycle of narcissism, you need to understand what the cycle of narcissism is and what role you play in this abuse system. The narcissistic cycle of abuse has four basic steps in it that enables narcissists to gain the admiration and attention they desire while keeping their sense of superiority over others. This calculated cycle helps them smear your name and keep you quiet while enabling them to keep going without ever getting caught.

The narcissistic abuse cycle starts with the narcissist feeling threatened, which causes them to abuse others while also positioning themselves as the victim. Through this, they feel empowered which enables them to feel superior before they begin feeling threatened all over again. What will threaten a narcissist varies from person to person, and can also vary from day to day. For example, sometimes, a narcissistic mother might feel threatened by their daughter looking prettier than they do because it gets the daughter more attention, whereas other times she might be fine with it because it makes her look good. There is never a way to truly tell what position she is going to take, which makes the narcissist mother volatile and frustrating to be around.

For the victim of the abuse or the daughter in this situation, it can feel like your mother builds you up and makes you feel great at times, only to tear you down again. After tearing you down she leaves you all but begging her for more positive attention, only to withhold it from you as a form of punishment. Then, when you finally give up and you have no energy left to fight, she throws you a small amount of attention to give you a reason to start fighting for her attention and admiration all over again. This cycle continues as you constantly do whatever you can just to receive those small scraps of positive attention from your mother, despite never knowing when they are coming or what might warrant them.

Surround Yourself with Supportive Outsiders

For you to truly prepare to break free from the aforementioned cycle, you need to make sure that you have surrounded yourself with a support team that can help you get through the challenging periods that you are about to face. You want to make sure that your support team is filled with people that you can trust, and that will help you feel safe and comforted during the process. They should be people that you can inform as to what is going on and what you plan on doing, and that will believe your experiences and support you in the process.

There are two types of people you should surround yourself with when it comes to leaving an abusive situation of any kind: friends and loved ones, and trained professionals. Both are going to help you navigate what you are about to face more effectively so that you can withstand the transition period that takes place between you breaking out of the cycle and feeling confident and comfortable where you stand after the fact.

Loved ones can be the more challenging part of your support system to create, as you truly need to make sure that the loved ones you rely on are going to be helpful and will support you in leaving the toxic situation. If you surround yourself with loved ones who are likely to side with your mother, or who will try to downplay the reality of your experiences, you might find yourself falling back into the cycle all over again because you are trusting someone who is unhelpful. If you have people in your social circle who will genuinely believe you and who will not attempt to pressure you into healing your relationship with your mom, rather than healing yourself from her abuse, choose these people to surround yourself with. Otherwise, focus on spending some time intentionally making new friends who you can surround yourself with. This may take some time, but if you do so intentionally you will find that you can create at least two or three strong connections with people who will serve as your support team through the transition period. Make sure these are friends you can keep long term, as you do not want to use anyone, nor do you want to attempt to create a false sense of connection just so you can leave an unhealthy relationship.

The people you surround yourself with who are considered loved ones, such as friends and family, are the ones who you are going to talk to about your experiences. It is a good idea to open up to them honestly about what you are going through and what you may face in the future so that they understand what you are experiencing. This way, if you do need someone to talk to or vent to during the process they do not feel blindsided by your request to talk about something heavy. As well, they can look out for you and help you identify possible patterns that may lead to you going back into the unhealthy relationship with your mother.

You also need to have professionals on your team,

as your loved ones are simply not going to be able to help with everything. Furthermore, attempting to rely on them for that emotional support too often can lead to you feeling codependent on them which can transition your problems into new relationships. Having a therapist on your support team can give you someone qualified to talk to about the deeper and heavier experiences that can also guide you to begin healing from your abuse. This is a great way to ensure that you are taking responsible action toward managing the pain and troubles you are facing due to your mom, and it is a good idea to do so as soon as you plan on healing from the relationship you share with your mother. We talk in great depth about how you can find a therapist and work with one in chapter 13, as I know the idea of working with a therapist can be terrifying for someone who is going through the process of healing from this type of abuse.

Prepare Yourself For The Emotional Experience

The final straw in preparing yourself for breaking free from the cycle of narcissistic abuse is preparing yourself for the emotional experience you are going to have throughout this process. Healing from any form of abuse is painful, sometimes to the point where it feels even more painful than enduring the abuse itself. This is because when you are within the abuse you enter "survival mode" which ultimately keeps you fairly numb to the greater picture of what is going on. While you certainly experience emotions, you do not experience them as deeply as you do when you finally start to come out of it. Furthermore, stepping out of the cycle is going to expose you to emotions you are afraid of: such as a fear of being punished for not doing what are "supposed to do" or the anxiety of standing on your own two feet when you are used to serving someone else. When you were a child, these experiences lead to massive punishment and experiences of neglect and abuse. As an adult, your mother may attempt to engage in these forms of punishment again, but the reality is that you are no longer at the mercy of her. You are no longer a young child living in her house and relying on her to feed you, clothe you, house you, and take care of your needs. As scary as it may feel now, you are capable of standing on your own two feet and building your own life away from your mother's abuse and neglect.

The best way to prepare yourself for the emotional aspect of breaking free is to read stories about other daughters who have done it. You may even be able to find an online support forum of other daughters' who have experienced it so that you can communicate with people who truly understand what it feels like to go through what you have gone through. Listening to other people's stories and hearing what they truly experienced will help you mentally brace yourself for what is coming so that the intense emotional experience does not come as a shock and create a traumatic relapse in your relationship.

Chapter 7

GETTING PERSPECTIVE

Once you have your foundation in place for you to begin taking steps toward breaking free from the abuse pattern, you need to focus on getting perspective on what you are going through. For me, perspective was the difference between blaming myself and feeling completely consumed by what I was going through and realizing that it was not my fault and there was a world beyond the abusive one my mother dragged me into.

When you have been exposed to narcissistic abuse from your mother since a young age, your entire perspective is shaped around what she pressured you to think. For this reason, it can be easy to get sucked into the anxiety and fear that comes with this chaotic perspective that never seems to have any clear sense of direction or rules around what it truly is, or isn't. The perspective of narcissists and therefore the perspective of their abusers is confusing, overwhelming, and always filled with uncertainty which can further increase your feelings of stress related to the situation. This chaotic energy becomes so consuming that you cannot see anything beyond it, both because you were groomed not to and because you are constantly just trying to figure things out. It's like being trapped in a puzzle and not knowing the way out, and never realizing that you now have the power to put the puzzle down and walk away from it entirely.

Gaining perspective helps you see your situation objectively and recognize each part of the situation for what it truly is. In many ways, it cultivates a deeper sense of awareness around the chaotic energy you have been experiencing and why it has been so all-consuming for all of these years. You will find that in doing this, you start to put the pieces of reality together and the concept that there is a reality beyond this confusing and painful web no longer seems so crazy.

Start Viewing Your Situation for What it Truly Is

The first thing you need to do to start gaining perspective in your experience is to start viewing the situation for what it truly is. Begin to see your relationship with your mother as being one that is dysfunctional and filled with abuse.

Pull yourself out of the perspective of being a daughter who is never good enough, or who constantly has to try to live up to your mother's unreasonable and unclear standards of who you should be. Stop trying to understand it from your mother's perspective, because it is never going to make sense: it is always going to shift just as soon as you think you have it figured out so that she can keep you on your toes and pleasing her as much as you can. Let go of the idea that this reality she has attempted to spin for you is one that you are required to live in, and stop trying to justify why she behaves the way she behaves.

Instead: begin to label everything accordingly. Identify yourself as being the victim of narcissistic abuse, and your mother as being a narcissist. Identify the trauma you experienced in your childhood, and the coping methods you used to deal with that trauma, as being the product of abuse, not the product of you being a bad kid.

If you can, begin to label the parts of the narcissistic abuse cycle in your relationship and develop an understanding as to how it plays out specifically in your relationship. The cycle itself is virtually always the same from relationship to relationship, but what specific topics or techniques your mother may use to get you to comply with her may vary. For example, my mother always used the topic of my beauty and my artistic talent to either make me feel inadequate or to make herself look better. Your mother may have used your fitness level, your knowledge, or any other talents or skills you may have against you or in favor of herself throughout your childhood and even now into your adult years.

When you can begin to identify these patterns, especially when you can start labeling them while they are in action as you actively experience them, it becomes easier for you to see them for what they are. This way, you can start distancing yourself from the distorted reality of your mother and start centering yourself in the truth, your truth.

Explain the Story from An Outsider's Perspective

A great way to begin practically and honestly building your perspective around your mother, your trauma, and the acts of abuse you have experienced is to explain the story from an outsider's perspective. This practice was particularly emotional for me as it forced me to face the reality of just how much abuse I had faced in my life and how numb I had become to most of it. Sure, it hurt, but I had become so used to it that it no longer hurt as bad as it should, and that piece reality itself was extremely painful.

To explain the story from an outsider's perspective, sit down with a journal and begin to write down your entire life story surrounding your mother. Write about the types of abuse you faced, the stories she told you, and the ways she treated you when it was just the two of you versus when other people were around. Also be sure to write down what you overheard her telling other people about you, and what she seemed to behave like when she believed you were not around. Get a full perspective around what was going on and write it from third person so that it feels like you are truly narrating your life story with your mother.

You might find that using this outside perspective helps you fully see and become aware of everything that was going on. Doing this, starting as early as your youngest memories, can help you put into perspective the abuse you have faced and the way it has affected you throughout your lifetime.

In doing this, I also encourage you to start thinking about how you might respond to someone else telling you these experiences. Treat yourself with the same level of respect, concern, compassion, and support that you would treat someone else who was going through what you have gone through. Learning to give yourself this level of care will help you begin to honor what you have truly come through and accepted the level of trauma that you have faced in your life. Truly accepting and admitting to those levels of trauma and the way they have affected you will help you begin to have compassion for yourself and develop a sense of self-awareness around your trauma which will prove to be extremely helpful in healing from it.

Keep the Reality in Mind When Making Your Exit

When you begin to take steps toward breaking free from your abuse cycle, you must keep this reality in mind. Keep your journal nearby and re-read it anytime you feel yourself getting pulled into your mother's distorted reality so that you can keep yourself focused on your recovery. The more you can reinforce your sense of reality, the less likely you will be to fall for her abuse and find yourself believing in her lies again. This is your best opportunity to free yourself from abuse and move forward without constant relapses and regressions into the cycle.

Chapter 8

VALIDATING YOURSELF

A s you begin to build your perspective around what you have gone through, you may find that you have a hard time believing in your perspective. Until now, your mother has taught you to believe in her and everything she tells you, even if you can compile a long list of evidence as to why she is wrong and why her sense of reality is distorted. Because of the way your mother has groomed you, you will find yourself believing in what she says even if what she says makes no sense.

Another thing you might feel when you start to develop your perspective is intense fear. I knew that in the past when I had my perspective and trusted in myself and my non-distorted sense of reality it leads to a lot of abuse when I was younger, which created a large amount of anxiety in my perspective as an adult. I had severe anxiety around believing in myself and believing in my sense of reality because I had always been told that I was wrong and if I chose to believe I wasn't then I was severely punished. Maybe the same happened for you, or something along those similar lines.

In addition to disproving your sense of reality, your mother also likely destroyed your ability to validate yourself in many other ways. Through forcing you to fight for her admiration and attention she may have left you feeling inadequate in several different ways in your life. She may have left you feeling inadequate in every way. How deep your traumas lie and where they lie will depend on your unique relationship with your mom, but a common experience between those who have been abused by narcissists is to have major struggles invalidating themselves. Regardless of what you struggle to validate yourself around, I can almost guarantee you experience this symptom.

You must begin to learn to validate yourself before you start the process of officially physically breaking free from the cycle of abuse with your mother so that as you go through the transition you can validate yourself. If you do not practice validating yourself first, you will find that as much as you want to break free you struggle to do so because you do not have her validation to help you do it. Even though this may sound illogical, the process of breaking free will distort your sense of logic as you will be deeply invested in your emotions which can lead you to defy logic altogether. This is exactly how abuse gets so far in the first place.

Start to Get to Know Yourself in A Deeper Way

One of the biggest ways that you can begin to validate yourself is through getting to know yourself more deeply. At this point, your knowledge in who you truly are maybe extremely limited as you have been fed your sense of identity by your mother and you have not had time to find out whether it was true or not due to her excessive demands. Spending time getting to know yourself helps you feel a greater sense of confidence in who you are so that you can validate yourself as you go through life. When you know who you are, it becomes easier to assert yourself to both yourself and others, effectively giving you a strong foundation for self-validation.

After an abusive relationship, you should always spend time getting to know yourself all over again, even if you think you already know yourself. Abusive relationships can majorly distort your sense of identity, especially when they start in childhood, and you do not want to find yourself holding onto a distorted sense of identity automatically because you never dug deeper. Focus on starting with the very basics, such as who you are, where you work, and what you like and dislike. From there, spend time getting to know yourself more intimately by behaving as if you were getting to know a brand new friend. Through affording yourself this level of attention to detail, you can give yourself the best opportunity to get to know who you truly are and begin validating that true version of yourself to yourself and others in your life.

Keep Your Promises to Yourself, Always

Part of being able to validate yourself is being able to trust yourself. Many of the different abusive strategies your mother has used against you in your life will have directly compromised your ability to trust in yourself, so you need to make this a priority. A big way that you can start creating a deeper sense of trust in yourself right now is through keeping your promises to yourself, always, such as the promises you make to yourself throughout this book. When you promise that you are going to get to know yourself better, for example, keep that promise and put the effort in.

Keep promises to yourself no matter how big or small they are because this starts to give you a sense of self-sufficiency. When you can keep promises to yourself, you realize that you are capable of doing things that are important to you which means that you are independent and capable of standing on your own two feet. This works the same as achieving goals does the more goals you achieve, the more you can achieve because the more you believe in yourself. Teach yourself that you are trustworthy and capable of making promises to yourself and keeping every single one.

Learn to Tell Yourself the Things You Need to Hear

When we seek validation from outside of ourselves, we are directly looking for someone to tell us something that we believe we need to hear from another individual. For example, if you start asking other people to tell you whether or not your work is well done because you want to hear that it is, you believe that your work is not good enough until someone else decides that this is true.

Constantly seeking validation from outside of yourself in the form of approval is a direct reflection of how narcissists abuse their victims, so understand that this is something you were taught to do from a very young age. Still, as an adult, it is your responsibility to change this behavior if you are going to be able to give yourself the best foundation to leap from to remove yourself from your mother's abuse.

When you find yourself searching for validation from outside of yourself, ask yourself what it is that you truly want to hear from someone else. What message are you looking for that you believe you need to receive from someone else for it to be true? Once you have discovered what that message is, begin affirming it to yourself as much as you need to for you to believe it to be true. This is a great step for actually, actively validating yourself in every area of your life.

Stop Judging Yourself and Your Feelings

When you struggle to validate yourself, one thing you likely notice is that you judge yourself and your feelings, likely in the same ways that your mother has judged you. This judgment comes from outside of yourself, much in the same way that validation has always come from outside of yourself. In a sense, this is you using external validation to validate why you are not good enough at something, which is essentially the same thing as looking outside of yourself for validation that you are good enough.

To start validating yourself more effectively, you

need to witness this judgment and stop using it as a way to punish yourself or put yourself down by validating why you are bad. Remember that this is validation coming from outside of yourself and that you do not need validation from outside of yourself because you can validate yourself. Then, begin to identify what you truly believe about what you were originally judging, such as a behavior or a feeling, and start affirming that to yourself. For example, if your mother judges you for wearing your hair down and you think you look pretty wearing it down, start wearing it down and validating to yourself that you like it and therefore it is pretty.

Practice Parenting Your Inner Child

A massive action step that you can begin taking toward healing yourself from your mother's narcissistic abuse is learning how to parent your inner child. In psychology, our inner child is that inner part of ourselves that still exists as an imprint from our childhood. This is the inner part of yourself that might still be afraid of the dark even if you behave bravely now, or that might believe in the boogie man even though as an adult you know he's not real. Despite how silly it might sound, this part of yourself is very real and continues to exist inside of yourself even though you are now a full-grown adult living your own life.

When you are abused, such as through narcissism, your inner child exists with a lot more than just a fear of the dark or a made-up monster that hides under your bed. Your inner child exists with fear around a very real abuser who may or may not still be a part of your adult life. If you have already broken ties with her, she may still have a grasp on the way you think and feel, or on the way other family members perceive you, even all of these years later, causing you to indirectly experience her abuse. In all of these scenarios, she is still affecting you which means your inner child is still terrified of being exposed to her abuse.

A great way to identify who your inner child is would be to recognize the difference between how you talk to a trusted person about your mother, versus how you act around your mother. For example, with my fiancé, I used to pinpoint exactly how my mother was abusive and what I should do to get away from it, but the minute she was around I would feel speechless and powerless. This was the difference between my adult self and my inner child.

Once you have identified your inner child, and you begin to see where the lines exist between who she is and who you are now, you can start to parent your inner child. This means you can talk to that part of yourself as if she is with you right now and you are parenting her in the ways that your mom never did. You can tell yourself "it's okay, I'm here now and I'm going to protect you" or "she can't hurt you anymore, I'm here to take care of you." Learning how to talk to your inner child in this way builds up your belief in yourself and helps this fearful part of yourself feel seen, protected, and validated by you. As a result, not only do you increase your sense of self-validation but you also create an opportunity for you to boost your confidence and your sense of self-esteem, making it even easier for you to grow and heal from your narcissistic mother.

Chapter 9

ACKNOWLEDGING YOUR PAIN

T he more you dig into the realization of what has happened to you and what you have gone through, and stop blocking it out and justifying the behaviors of your mother, the more pain you are likely to experience. Coming into this process, you were already experiencing the pain of your mother's abuse, but it may start to feel like it is stinging even more as you begin to fully acknowledge it and accept what has happened to you over the years. It may start to feel like you are unraveling many pieces of your story that you kept blocked out or hidden for fear of having to face the growing amounts of pain that were accumulating in your life. As you do, this pain can all come up at once and it can be incredibly challenging. What's worse is you may be tempted to numb it out again or justify it in favor of your mother and her behaviors because this is how she has groomed you to act in order to continue serving her abusive patterns, by keeping you the victim.

I will repeat what I have already said a few times here, but this is where it is really important that you become aware of what you are experiencing and you consciously work through it. This is the point where I would always become overwhelmed by emotion and I would backtrack into a relapsed relationship with my mother because I was too afraid to go through the pain of being in this state. The problem with each backtracks was that each time I realized more about the truth of what I was living and it became harder to numb everything out and stay trapped in the abuse. As I continued to realize how toxic and dangerous these behaviors were, I found myself feeling even more traumatized by each succeeding episode of abuse. At this point, not only was I being traumatized by my mothers' abuse but I was also being traumatized by my seeming inability to get beyond it.

I want to help you avoid this repetitive cycle I found myself in and fully release yourself from this abuse pattern so that you can avoid the intense trauma that comes with the back-and-forth of trying to escape. The better you can prepare yourself for this and work through it, the better your chances are going to be for you to fully remove yourself from the situation and truly begin healing yourself and your life. Understand that this does not mean you are not going to experience trauma or the painful reality of your previous trauma, but it will hopefully help you avoid compounding your trauma with additional traumatizing experiences.

At this point in your journey, if you have not already you should begin distancing yourself from your mother. While you go through this painful acknowledgment you do not want to have your mother exercising her narcissistic tools to attempt to pull you back in, leaving you feeling even more confused and overwhelmed. You truly want to be as removed from the situation as possible so that you can rely on yourself and your sense of reality to help guide you through the healing process. As you go through this distancing there will be even more pain relating to the distancing itself that comes up, so be prepared to be patient with yourself and move at a pace that fits what you can reasonably handle. It is perfectly safe to take this all at your own pace, as attempting to rush any step can lead to you feeling overwhelmed and regressing into the victim mindset which will keep you trapped in the cycle even longer.

Know Where Your Pain Truly Comes From

The first thing you need to do when you are acknowledging the pain you are experiencing is taking the time to understand where your pain truly comes from. Daughters of narcissistic mothers can almost always draw their pain points back to their mothers, as their mothers tend to infect every area of their lives with toxic words and beliefs. You might go so far as to find that the pain you experience from being too afraid to go for it in your dream career is because your mother taught you that you were not worthy enough or smart enough to do anything meaningful with your life.

It can be painful and even shocking to realize that much of the pain you have experienced in your life fall back on the way your mother treated you and the way she taught you to believe about yourself. With that being said, you need to get honest about where your pain is coming from and what started this pain in the first place. Every time you feel any level of pain in any area of your life, especially emotionally or mentally, you need to pause and look at where this pain truly comes from. Pinpoint the moment in your history that this pain started, and do your best to remember everything about the situation that caused this pain. Also take note of any subsequent events that reinforced this pain, as these recurring events will have encouraged the pain to become even worse and will also need to be healed.

Knowing where your pain comes from down to the exact moments that caused it and reinforced it is going to help you move forward from them. Now, rather than internalizing the beliefs your mother fed you in those moments, such as you not being good enough or capable enough, you can recall the truth. You feel this pain not because you are truly not good enough, but because you were bullied by your mother into believing that to be true. With this in mind, you can start to heal from the abuse of your mother, rather than staying in the mindset of constantly trying to "fix" yourself to be a better person because your mother has to lead you to believe that you are somehow broken.

Label the Pain You Experience

Individuals who have become victims of narcissistic abuse often have a hard time identifying their exact emotions. Throughout your life, you have been consumed with attempting to understand and navigate your mother's emotions, to the point where you may not have any clear understanding as to what emotion feels like within yourself. I know for myself the only emotions I ever recall experiencing until I began healing from my relationship with my mother were anxiety and anger. I would constantly switch back and forth between the anxiety of what abuse would come next and the anger at my mother for not being able to be a better parent to me. At that point, I had no idea that I was also experiencing grief, fear, guilt, sadness, disappointment, overwhelm, trauma, and many other emotions that link to being involved in an abusive mother-daughter relationship.

Learning how to properly label your emotions is going to help you start to know and understand yourself better, and it is also going to teach you to think about yourself. Until now, you have not had much time to think about yourself because you have always been thinking about your mother and what your mother's needs are. Being in that position has likely been incredibly painful, and has led to you feeling your inner sense of self-neglect because you have let yourself and your life be overruled by your mother and her never-ending needs.

I found that the more I learned to properly label my emotions, the more liberated I felt. I began to understand every single emotion I was experiencing, and I was able to truly address those emotions in a way that was more appropriate to what they were. I was also able to start feeling normal for perhaps the first time in my entire life because I realized that my emotions were a natural response to my abuse. I no longer felt like I was bad or wrong for feeling any of these things, but that I was incredibly healthy and normal for having these emotional responses to my upbringing. For the first time in my life, I felt like I had a hope of being someone other than the abused daughter of a narcissistic mother.

The best tip I learned to help me identify my own emotions was to use a wheel of emotions. My therapist gave me this tool to help me identify my emotions, and it works by starting in the center to identify the most basic emotion you are feeling, like "sadness". For example, I was feeling sad because I feel like my mother does not love me, and that made me sad. Then, you follow the wheel out to properly identify what type of sadness you are feeling, until you reach a more definitive emotion, like feeling inferior or isolated, both of which were true for me. When you begin to have these exact emotions that describe how you feel, it becomes clearer as to why you feel the way you do and your ability to start allowing yourself to process these emotions becomes easier, too. Now, rather than feeling confused and overwhelmed by your emotions, you feel aware of and understanding in them.

Keep A Journal of Your Feelings

I strongly advise you to keep a journal as you go through this entire experience and that in that journal you regularly write down how you are feeling. At least a few times per day, and every time you feel an overwhelming influx of emotions, stop to identify what exact emotions you are feeling. You may find that you are being overwhelmed by just one emotion, or you may find you are being overwhelmed by many. There is no right or wrong answer, simply write down everything you are feeling and the symptoms of those emotions that you are feeling.

Then, write down where that emotion comes from, and how you can navigate that emotion now as an adult. Part of navigating that emotion now will likely include accepting that it exists, searching for healthier ways to express that emotion, and allowing yourself to work through it so that you can fully release it.

A real example from my emotion journal looks just like this:

"I feel jealous because my friend Judy has a mother that is so attentive and caring. She calls her every week and they share a great relationship with each other. I know

this comes from my mother never sharing that with me, and the realization that we never will. This jealousy makes me feel nauseous, angry, and like crying over what I will never have. I am choosing to accept that this is my reality, and I am going to use this acceptance to help me move through this jealousy. I know my broken relationship with my mother is not my fault, and the feeling will not last forever, and I am ultimately happy to know that Judy gets to share such a great relationship with her mother. It makes me happy to see that this type of love exists in her life, even if it does not exist in mine."

Taking the time to write like this on your own emotions will help you see what your emotions truly are, validate them, and healthily process them. This way, you can move through them and release them, allowing you to make room for more enjoyable emotions like gratitude and acceptance.

Chapter 10

LEARNING TO MEET YOUR OWN NEEDS

Part of healing from your mother's narcissism is learning to meet your own needs. The average person learns to identify and meet their own needs as a child, but daughters raised by narcissistic mothers do not have the privilege of doing this. Rather than spending time learning how to identify and understand their own emotions, they spend their entire childhoods learning to identify and understand their mother's emotions. Of course, they never succeed because their mother's emotions are so volatile and ever-changing, but they will do their best to try, anyway.

As an adult, this behavior likely pours into your other relationships with you naturally thinking about everyone else before yourself. I did this to the point where it was so automatic that I did not even realize

I was doing it until it was done and then I realized my own needs had gone unmet. Then, I would grow incredibly frustrated and resentful to the people in my life for not choosing to see and meet my needs in the way that I had been doing for them. Of course, they were not doing this because this was not a form of healthy or normal behavior, but I had no idea that this was a behavior that was unique to me as a result of my abuse. Not until I started to look into my symptoms and heal from my narcissistic mother, anyway.

Learning how to heal from your mother's abuse and function normally as an independent adult requires you to learn how to see, and meet, your own needs before anyone else's. You have likely heard the phrase before, which states: "you cannot serve from an empty vessel" by Eleanor Brown. When I heard this, it resonated deeply, yet I was not yet aware of how to put this advice into action in my own life. It took a lot of time learning how to discover what my needs were, and teaching myself to identify these needs in a timelier manner and communicate them with assertiveness before overwhelming myself with the needs of others.

As you continue to heal, you need to learn how to make this switch, too. You need to learn how to identify what your needs are and assertively communicate them before you agree to take on anything that would defy your own needs.

Learn How to Identify Your Needs

I found that the biggest secret to identifying my own needs was tapping into my inner dialogue and using it intentionally. In the past, I had ignored my inner dialogue to attempt to consider what my mothers' needs were, which meant my thoughts always revolved around her.

My inner voice sounded a lot like this:

- "What does my mother need?"
- "What will make my mother happy?"
- "How can I keep my mother from getting angry?"
- "How can I please my mother?"
- "What can I do to keep myself from being neglected?"

Every single thought revolved around my mother. When I moved out of her home, the thoughts like that continued, both around the topic of my mother and the topic of anyone else I cared about. Like you, I was taught that respect and love were shown by abnormal levels of appreciation to the point where the person you respect and love is almost the only thing you think about.

Except, that's not healthy.

I began to tap into my inner dialogue and intentionally change my thoughts as I went through my day. Every time I found myself asking about how I could serve my mother, or someone else, I would instead ask how I could serve myself. This would require me to know my own needs, which meant it started the inner dialogue around identifying those needs and understanding them.

At first, identifying your own needs is going to feel strange. You might find yourself feeling guilty and selfish for thinking about yourself, and you might feel bad or wrong for not thinking about others. You may think that they are going to believe you do not love them or care about them if you do not put them first before yourself, because you have been taught that this is the only true way to show your love for someone else. This is not true, and the reality is that most people are not going to want to have you put their needs and desires before yours. In many ways, this makes it feel like you are putting too much pressure on them or attaching them into an unhealthy way, which leads to them not wanting to be around you as much. Alternatively, it could drive you directly into the path of more narcissists and abusers because you are already perfectly groomed to be taken advantage of by them.

As you continue to have this inner dialogue, however, you will start to understand that your own needs are separate from the needs of others. You will come to realize that there is no reason for you to feel responsible for other people's needs because meeting their needs is their responsibility. Meeting your needs is your own (and only) responsibility. And, of course, if you have a younger child of your own then meeting their needs is your responsibility to, to the point that is appropriate for their age.

Create Rituals for Fulfilling Your Needs

Something you can try that might help you begin to take care of your own needs first is creating rituals or habits around how you fulfill your own needs. Rituals that are designed to help you fulfill your own needs can help you turn this into a habit, rather than something that you have to fight to remember to do. It can also make fulfilling your habits feel more fun and enjoyable, making it easier for you to convince yourself that it is worth your while.

The three rituals I keep for myself that help me fulfill my own needs include a ritual for identifying my needs, a ritual for daily stress management, and a ritual to put myself in a positive mood whenever I am feeling down. My ritual for identifying my own needs is truly a simple conversation I have with myself that reminds me to check in and understand myself and my own needs before I commit to anything. My ritual I have for stress management is a bath with a candle, and some time spent feeling my emotions and validating myself. I use this one a lot after my mother has attempted any abusive cycle, as it helps me remember that I am worthy and valuable, despite how she may attempt to make me feel. Lastly, my ritual for helping myself feel better is to put on my favorite music and dance to it for five to ten minutes, no matter how I am feeling when I start. This helps raise my energy and put me in a good mood every single time.

You can decide what rituals you need in your own life to help you meet your own needs and feel better continually. I strongly recommend making them something that feels fun and fulfilling for you, as this will help you genuinely honor your own needs and start taking care of yourself. Even starting by learning to fulfill a few needs at a time can help you grow and have a better experience with managing your own needs first over anyone else's. As you begin to make this a more positive and enjoyable experience, you will find it becomes easier over time.

Permit Yourself to Come First

Although this entire practice of learning to fulfill your own needs has involved you learning to put yourself first, you must pause and give yourself intentional permission to come first. Giving yourself verbal permission to choose you over anyone else is a powerful opportunity for you to take this from a "good idea" and turn it into an actual practice that you are going to use in your life. When you commit to taking things and turning them into an action plan, your life begins to change much faster.

A great way to start permitting yourself to come first, and a great way to remind yourself that you have done so, is to create a mantra around permitting yourself to come first. I made mine as simple as possible, with it saying: "I give myself permission to come first." I repeat this to myself every time I notice I have a need that needs to be met, and then I go through the process of understanding what that need is and how I can reasonably meet it at that very moment.

Chapter 11

SETTING STRONG BOUNDARIES

As you might have guessed, part of being involved in a narcissistic mother-daughter relationship is not knowing how to assert boundaries. Overstepping natural boundaries and making you feel like you had nothing that truly belonged to you or that was yours was one of your mother's ways of making you put her first over everything in your life. By doing this, she was able to essentially hijack your brain and make you think about her and her needs over you and your own at all times.

Not having learned boundaries in your childhood can lead to you finding yourself in many situations as an adult where you struggle to assert your boundaries. This very experience may have affected nearly every human interaction you have had in your life until this point. Situations with your other family members, friends, lovers, co-workers, bosses, and even acquaintances may have all lead to you being taken advantage of or treated poorly at one time or another because you did not know how to assert your boundaries. Furthermore, you might have felt at various times that learning to do so would be rude, as you would be directly showing a sign of disrespect or ungratefulness by learning to assert boundaries. You may not realize that there is such thing as positive boundaries that can be asserted politely, or that these boundaries are something that you are allowed to exercise in your life.

It is time for you to begin learning how to assert your boundaries in a polite yet stern manner that will ensure that anyone who hears you asserting your boundaries know you mean business. This will help you stop over-giving and being taken advantage of, and it will prevent others from seeing you as someone that can be taken advantage of. It will also help you finally put an end to the painful question of: "why is everyone else being treated better by this person, except me?" A question that is commonly asked by victims of narcissistic abuse who have yet to learn how to assert themselves and their boundaries.

Learn How to Say "No"

One of the first things you need to teach yourself when you are learning to set and assert boundaries is the word "no." As a daughter of a narcissist, you have been taught that "no" is not only an unacceptable word but also a dangerous word. In your childhood, you were likely punished in major ways, including being berated or neglected, for using the word "no" with your mother. She may have even smeared you to other people by painting herself as the victim any time you attempted to say no to her. Whatever measures she took, you have likely learned that saying no is dangerous and not ideal in any circumstance, ever.

What you did not realize as a child was that almost no one reacts this way. Having an excessive or exaggerated response to the word "no" is not normal, or healthy, and it is also not common. Most people will not be abusive to you if you say no to them. I'm guessing that you may have realized this at various points in your life, but that you still find yourself feeling overly sensitive every time someone shows any signs of disappointment when you say no. This is because you have been taught that their feelings are your responsibility, through the unhealthy expectations of your mother.

In learning to say no, you need to learn that it is A) appropriate and healthy to say no, and B) it is not your responsibility to manage other people's emotions. You need to exercise your new skills of fulfilling your own needs and use the word "no" as a way to do so consistently, whenever you need to. By practicing using the word "no" anytime you find yourself in a situation where you are being asked to do something that makes you feel as though your own needs are going unfulfilled, you will start reinforcing both your needs and your boundaries. This will make doing both much easier going forward.

Be Direct, Yet Polite When Asserting Yourself

A big fear that daughters of narcissistic mothers have when it comes to setting boundaries is the belief that no matter how you do it, asserting your boundaries is a sign of ignorance and a lack of love and respect. When you learn to assert yourself, it can be helpful to realize that asserting your boundaries is a sign of love for both yourself and the other person, as you are valuing the healthy relationship you share with them. The only way you can do that is if you value yourself and your health, which comes with asserting your needs and your boundaries.

You can help yourself begin to see boundaries as a positive thing by realizing that there are ways to politely assert your boundaries that are still direct and effective. By using the direct yet polite approach, you can start to rebuild your beliefs around what boundaries are and how they serve you in your life.

A great direct yet polite way of asserting your boundaries would be as simple as saying: "No thank you" when someone asks if you want to do something. If they continue to pressure you, you can say "I have asserted my boundary by saying no thank you, please stop." If they continue further, you can say "I do not feel that you are respecting me, I am going to end this conversation now." This is not disrespectful but is instead a sign of you loving yourself and asserting your boundaries and needs. In this, you did not berate or disrespect anyone, but you did show love and respect to yourself, which means that it is a positive and healthy example of setting boundaries.

It is important that when you do issue a consequence of what will happen if your boundaries continue to be ignored that you follow through. Not following through on your consequences will result in people not believing in you and your boundaries, which will lead to them continually overstepping your boundaries no matter how hard you attempt to assert them. This is because you have taught them that your boundaries ultimately do not mean anything and that you can be taken advantage of, despite you trying to avoid this. You need to be assertive and remain assertive, including by following through on your promised actions, to show people that you are not willing to be taken advantage of. In doing so, people will either leave you alone or learn to treat you in a way that is more appropriate to how you desire to and deserve to, be treated.

Create A System of Personal Rules (And Follow Them)

Creating boundaries in your life when you are not used to having boundaries in your life can be a difficult experience. At this point, you may have absolutely zero boundaries that you are regularly asserting in your life, which may make you feel like you have to start from scratch because, in a sense, you do. It can be overwhelming to look at all areas of your life and realize that your lack of boundaries leaves you vulnerable and susceptible to people's mistreatment. You could start to feel like there are a lot of areas of your life that need to be addressed to avoid letting people, like your mother, take advantage of you any further.

When I was first learning to assert my boundaries, I chose to create a system of personal rules and then apply them in every situation where boundaries were needed. These personal rules helped me identify my needs and desires, and then assert my boundaries to help me ensure that my needs and desires were fulfilled. They also helped me keep my boundaries with myself by not breaking my rules and letting people, including me, take advantage of myself. This way, I was confident that I would treat myself with the level of respect that I deserved and that I would ensure everyone else would too if they desired to be in my life and presence.

Creating personal rules for yourself can help give you a guideline of healthier practices to follow in your day to day life. This way, you can step away from the toxic behaviors your mother taught you when you were growing up, such as not to have or assert your boundaries, and start living a healthier life.

The rules you create should reflect who you are, what you desire from life, how you desire to get it, and what makes you feel your best in your everyday experience. They can involve how you are willing to treat yourself and how you are willing to let others treat yourself, how you are going to make decisions that serve you, and anything else that genuinely helps you live a better quality of life.

Some of my own life rules include:

1. I will not let anyone take advantage of me or overstep my boundaries.
2. I will always put my own needs before anyone else's.
3. I will not do anything that does not ultimately make me feel happy, loved, or supported.
4. I will only allow healthy, non-toxic relationships to exist in my life.
5. I will not let anyone minimize or devalue the experiences I have.
6. My perception of reality is my truth, and no one can tell me otherwise.
7. I will validate myself and not seek validation from others.
8. I will not place my value on the perception that others have of me.
9. My own happiness and wellbeing is the most important thing in my life.
10. I am not required to go out of my way to fulfill others' needs.

You should make your list of rules in your journal that you can use and reflect on to help you begin identifying your needs and asserting your boundaries. I suggest reading that list every single day to remind you of who you are and what you will and will not allow happening in your life. Then, to the best of your ability, uphold all of those rules on a day to day basis. The more you do, the more empowered you will feel to take control over your life and stop letting other people take advantage of you.

Chapter 12

CHOOSING FORGIVENESS

I'm not going to lie: I have declared that many parts of this process are going to be challenging because they are. Healing from narcissism is not easy in any sense of the experience, and virtually every step is going to have a level of difficulty to it as you face the reality of what you have come through and teach yourself to be a healthy, functioning member of society.

The forgiveness part of the healing process offers its unique type of pain and confusion, however, and I want to highlight that before we dig into it. When you reach the point where it is time for you to begin forgiving people for the pain, they have caused you, and yourself for the ways you have contributed, you reach a point where you truly need to commit to changing your perspective. At this point, you need to accept that you are removed from the situation and admit that you are ready to see things differently. You are ready to see things with a loving, compassionate perspective that encompasses having love and compassion for yourself, too.

Forgiveness is often seen by victims as a way to justify what the abuser has done and, in some way, declare that what they did no longer matters, or that the pain no longer exists. Staying in this mindset can keep you feeling troubled and confused around the topic of forgiveness because it may feel like you are attempting to erase or justify everything your mother has done to you in your life. Another angle here is that if you decide everything, she did in the past is now "okay" then in some ways you are admitting that her repeated abusive behaviors are somehow "okay", too. After all, how can something be considered okay in the past but not okay in the future? This perspective is one I know all too well, and it is one that can add to the confusion and inner turmoil around trying to forgive your mother.

As you ponder on the topic of forgiveness, you may also start to feel an intense sense of overwhelming. Maybe you feel that some things will be easier to forgive, but others will not be. Understand that forgiving your mother does not have to be done all at once, as blanket forgiveness does not have to be issued. You can choose to forgive one thing at a time as they come up, while also choosing to forgive the experiences you have had in your life until now.

One last toxic perspective I want to address is if you feel like you have something new to forgive every day and so you are in a chronic state of having to attempt to forgive your mother for everything she continues to do. If this is how you are feeling about the topic of forgiveness, understand that in this experience you are not truly forgiving your mother but instead you are using forgiveness as a way to enable her to continue behaving in a toxic manner. You are not required to forgive her and enable her to continue treating you in the same way that warranted forgiveness in the first place. You can exercise forgiveness with boundaries so that you can have your needs met and distance yourself from her abusive behaviors. That is a choice you can make, and it is also a choice I recommend that you do make. Doing so will prove to you that forgiveness is truly an act of self-love, and not an enabling or minimizing behavior that is meant to take away your right to being outraged and hurt by how you have been treated.

With all that being said, forgiveness is a crucial step in healing. Forgiveness is a step that enables you to choose to no longer give power to the painful things people have done to you, including yourself, and instead give the power back to yourself so that you can heal those wounds. When you forgive someone, you decide that you are going to accept the situation as it is and place your energy on becoming aware of your pain so you can heal it, rather than placing your energy and hate and revenge toward the person that hurt you. Forgiving is a way of letting yourself off the hook so that you can begin to make changes in your life by asserting loving boundaries and moving on from the situations that hurt you in the first place.

Learn to Forgive Your Mother in Your Way

The very first phase of forgiveness you need to begin with is learning how to forgive your mother. Your mother is the person who hurt you first, and who likely hurt you deepest. She is the person who filled your heart with disappointment, rejection, abandonment, fear, neglect, sorrow, grief, guilt, shame, and many other painful emotions that you live with every day. She is the one who ultimately let you down and failed to provide you with the safe, loving, and nourishing childhood that every child deserves to experience, and requires to thrive and grow into a healthy, functioning adult. The reason why you are here right now reading this book and healing from this in the first place is because of your mother and her behaviors.

Your mother is the source of much of your pain, and she has used this pain to feel powerful over you for most of your life. By keeping you in this state of pain, and by you allowing it, you are letting your mother continue to control you even when she is not around to control you through her active words and actions. Her voice rings through your head and reminds you of all of her moments of cruelty and keeps you down, preventing you from being able to fully heal.

Choosing to forgive your mother in your way means finding the balance between forgiving her for not being able to be a better mother to you, and setting strong loving boundaries that prevent her toxic behaviors from impacting you anymore. How this looks exactly is going to depend on what feels right for you, and where that balance lies for you between forgiveness and boundaries.

The reason why forgiveness specifically is important here is that when you switch into a perspective of having forgiveness for your mother, you also have compassion for her. This compassion supports you with releasing the feelings that are associated with your pain so that you can let go of that pain as you begin to heal through it. As a result, you are not creating more pain for yourself every time you think about your mother or the experiences you two have shared, or not shared. Having healthy boundaries in place will ensure that this compassion is not used against you. For example, with boundaries in place you are less likely to be compassionate to the point where you justify her behaviors and allow her to continue treating you in this poor manner. This way, you can release the pain without exposing yourself to more abuse and trauma in the process.

Forgive Yourself for Your Experiences

Another person you need to forgive in this experience is yourself. You need to understand that for most of your life you were young and unable to speak up for yourself, and during those years your mother wrongfully took advantage of you and taught you not to speak up for yourself. This way, as an adult, you would be less likely to speak up and end the cycle of abuse which would ultimately enable her to continue behaving this way.

You are not responsible for how your mother treated you, or for how you were groomed as a child to comply with her unreasonable demands as an adult. It is not your fault that your mother has a mental condition, or that this mental condition affected you and caused you to adopt unhealthy behaviors and coping methods at various points throughout your life. Even though you may feel ashamed of how these behaviors or coping methods have affected your relationship or reputation with others, it is not your fault that this happened. When it was happening, you had no idea that this was not the "appropriate" way to act, because to you this was the only appropriate way to navigate the incredible amounts of pain and abuse your mother was exposing you to daily. Most people who judged you had no idea what was truly going on and those who did likely had no way of comprehending how bad it was due to the way your mother expertly hid her abuse through grooming you and others not to see it when it happened.

Accepting this all to be true is a powerful opportunity for you to forgive yourself, which will help you stop blaming yourself and punishing yourself for the ways you have acted in the past. You can accept that you did not know better at the time and that the way people treated or viewed you due to your behavior was not because you were bad or wrong, but because neither of you truly understood what was happening. You had no way of knowing that your behaviors would be seen as abnormal or strange by others, and they had no way of knowing what you were truly going through that caused you to behave that way. It was not your fault that your mother treated you that way or that others did, and so you need to forgive yourself.

As you forgive yourself, learn to have compassion for yourself and all that you have been through, and all that you did to cope with it. Also learn how to have boundaries with yourself so that you no longer allow yourself to continue punishing or blaming yourself for these things, or otherwise reinforcing the pain and trauma through your own words, thoughts, or behaviors. Learn to release and let go, and set a boundary that permits you to become a new person, with new coping methods and behaviors, today. Commit to moving forward more healthily, and watch how much this level of forgiveness transforms your relationship with yourself, and your life in general.

Choose to Forgive Those Who Didn't Believe You

The final area of forgiveness you need to focus on is forgiving those who did not believe you or what you were going through. People who chalked your pain or abuse up to being a "typical mother-daughter relationship" or to you being overdramatic had no way of knowing what was truly going on because your mother expertly hid it from them. Or, maybe they experienced similar traumas from their mother and have not yet come to terms with it or learned to view abuse for what it truly is. Maybe they carry their unhealthy perspectives on what a healthy relationship should look like, and how love and respect are shown to others.

When it comes to forgiving and healing from your narcissistic abuse, forgiving others will also help prevent you from holding them to blame for what you went through. It will also help you stop punishing them in your mind for not being able to help you or validate you, which will support you in ending the cycle of painful emotions relating to your mother's abuse. Make sure that in forgiving others, you learn to have compassion for them while also having boundaries with them. Do not forgive others and allow them to continue minimizing the pain you carry or the level of abuse you experienced, or otherwise downplaying what you went through. After you have forgiven them, assert boundaries around what you are and are not willing to discuss with them, and reserve your right to withhold discussions about your mother with anyone who cannot respect what you went through. You are not obligated to let people judge or pass opinions to you based on what you went through, no matter who that person may be.

Chapter 13

WORKING WITH THERAPISTS

Whenever you are healing from any form of abuse, I always advise that you work with a qualified therapist who can help you completely heal from the abuse you have faced in your life. Especially in a situation that is as complex as healing from narcissism, having a therapist can help you work through the challenging emotions and realizations and have compassion for yourself. They can also support you in developing healthier coping methods and self-care routines while keeping you accountable in your commitment to living a healthier life.

I always recommend the route I went when I finally removed myself from my narcissistic mother's abusive cycle, which was to combine self-help with professional therapists. I read as much as I could, surrounded myself with supportive people, and did everything I could to inform and educate myself on what I was going through and how I could successfully get through it. Then, I also hired a professional therapist who could help me in ways that I could not help myself and that would not available through my loved ones or books. My therapist has helped me understand my unique situation, create custom strategies for healing and coping based on my personal needs, and has ultimately supported me in feeling safe and comfortable during the entire experience.

Hiring a therapist can seem scary, especially if you have had a negative experience with one. Personally, in my childhood, my school connected me with a childhood therapist who ended up speaking with my mother behind my back which resulted in her believing I was lying and in need of help for being a chronic liar, rather than a child that was being abused. It took me some time to heal from this and confide in a new therapist, but I am grateful that I did. My therapist now in adulthood is private, only communicates with me, and is fully committed to helping me get through my challenges relating to my mother and many other things in my life at this point. Remember that you are now an adult and that your mother does not have the power to negatively influence your access to help, and that you are entitled to receiving the help that you need.

Self-Validate Your Right to Seek Help

Right now, is an excellent time for you to practice self-validation as you validate to yourself that you have a right to seek help and that you are deserving of the help you desire. Use this as an opportunity to prove your commitment to yourself and your needs, to assert boundaries in your mind to the thoughts that tell you that you do not need help, and to forgive yourself for your fears around help. You can even use this as a time to label and work through the emotions you are having around the idea of hiring a therapist in the first place to seek help.

Whatever it takes for you to commit to finding and working with a therapist and getting help, I strongly advise you do. While I cannot force you to go see anyone, I also cannot stress enough how much having a therapist has transformed my ability to completely move beyond the trauma my mother inflicted upon me throughout my lifetime. I meet with my therapist monthly, and I always meet with her before and after I see my mother as this ensures I stay on track with my healing. My therapist has helped me hold myself accountable in countless experiences, and when you are healing from abuse, especially abuse that started before you could even talk, this is so important. Please consider getting yourself a therapist to help you through this.

Find A Trauma-Informed Therapist

In finding a therapist, I want to point out that you need to find a trauma-informed therapist. These days, many therapists make an effort to be trauma-informed which means that there should be no shortage of therapists available to you to help you with what you are going through. With that being said, do make sure that when you are looking for a therapist you ask them what sorts of the trauma, they have helped people heal from, and what their philosophies on healing from trauma are. You can also ask them about their experience with narcissism specifically. Knowing that your therapist understands your unique type of trauma and what you might be going through can help assure yourself that they are going to believe you and be helpful to your healing experience. This may help you feel more confident in actually attending your therapy appointments and opening up to your therapist, too.

Create A Sense of Safety in Your Client-Therapist Relationship

Always make sure that when you work with a therapist you pick one who helps you feel safe and supported right from day one. It might be challenging to tell if you are particularly afraid of visiting a therapist in general, but typically you will know because you will speak with a therapist who seems to help you feel better. You want to pick a therapist who helps you feel more comfortable and supported from the start, as this is a therapist that you are likely to develop a good relationship with. If you find you have a therapist who you do not feel comfortable with, recognize that this is likely a mismatch between you and your therapist's personality and not evidence that therapy will not help you.

If you do have fear around visiting your therapist, even if you think that fear sounds silly or strange, do not be afraid to open up about this. You could even make this your first area of focus so that you can test the waters to see how your therapist responds to your emotions and your needs. In many instances, sharing this will help you feel more confident and will allow your therapist to understand your needs while also showing you that they are there to help you, not judge or hurt you.

Lastly, I recommend keeping the topic of your therapist away from your mother unless you truly feel the need to tell her. I did not tell my mother about my therapist for years, and I have never discussed why I am in therapy with her. Telling your mother that you go to therapy, or telling her that you go because of her, could expose you to being abused by your mother for your choice which could compromise your willingness to continue going. Some things are better kept to yourself, and this is often one of those things. You can do so by asserting the boundary that you are not required to tell your mother everything can be incredibly helpful in establishing a sense of security in your client-therapist relationship.

Chapter 14

EVALUATING OTHER RELATIONSHIPS

An unfortunate experience that many victims of childhood abuse from a narcissist have is that they begin to experience abuse from other people in their lives. These other people seem to sense that they can withstand abuse and that they will do so without asserting boundaries or walking away because they truly do not know how to protect themselves. As a result, they become the victims of all sorts of abuse throughout their lives, to the point where they may wonder why they are the "chosen ones" to be victims in so many different ways.

If you have been involved in an abusive relationship with a narcissist in your life, there is a good chance that you have experienced abuse, or at least abusive behaviors, in other areas of your life, too. Being groomed from childhood to remain open and vulnerable to your mother's abuse means that you are more vulnerable to other abusive people's abuse, too. Other abusers will recognize that you are incapable of protecting yourself and will use this to their advantage by turning you into their victim as well, leaving you exposed to multiple forms of abuse.

Being exposed in this way and enduring the abuse from many people can leave you feeling many different things. You will likely begin to experience an incredibly low sense of self-worth, self-esteem, and self-confidence as it feels like many people in your life are harming you. You may also struggle to believe that there are any good people in the world because you are constantly wrapped up in cycles of abuse with various people who leave you feeling like the only thing that exists is pain and abuse.

Furthermore, you might carry that lack of trust into any positive or healthy relationship that does begin to form in your life, resulting in you self-sabotaging that relationship and losing it. When this begins to happen, you may even start blaming yourself for why you are not in better relationships, which can further worsen your experiences in the relationships in your life. You might begin to think that your inability to maintain healthy relationships means that it is entirely your fault that you are not in any healthy relationship, and that you deserve to be trapped in these abusive relationships you are a part of. Of course, this is not true, but this is a highly common cycle for abuse victims to go through, which can lead them to stay in unhealthy relationships even if they think they know better.

Reflect On Your Existing Relationships

The first thing you need to do when evaluating your relationships is reflected in your existing relationships. Consider who your top 2-5 friends are, or who you spend most of your time with, and reflect on the relationships you share with these people. Pay attention to important things such as how you feel around these people and how they treat you. Consider them against your list of personal rules, particularly the rules around how you are willing to let other people treat you, and see how they compare. Are they generally treating you in a way that is healthy and kind? Or are they treating you in a way that violates your new personal rules, and boundaries?

In addition to considering the other person, consider how you behave in these relationships. Are you behaving like a healthy individual as a part of these relationships, or are you contributing to the relationship in a negative, unhealthy manner? You might realize that you are behaving in a way that results in you taking responsibility for their emotions and behaviors, which is unhealthy. In this case, their unhealthy behaviors may not necessarily be a reflection of them, but instead, it may be a reflection of how you have taught them to treat you. In doing so, you may have allowed them to treat you poorly and they may have gone along with it without truly realizing that this is what they were doing.

Be objective when you are reflecting on your relationships so that you can place responsibility where it belongs. In other words, you need to take responsibility for your actions, but do not take responsibility for theirs. Even if their actions are a response to your actions, hold them accountable for how they treat you so that you can contribute to a healthier dynamic in your relationship with them.

Learn to Create Healthier Relationship Dynamics

Upon reflecting on your relationships, you are also going to want to learn new ways to engage in relationships in a healthier way. You want to make sure that in the relationships where healthier dynamics can be achieved, you work toward achieving them. You can do so through asserting your boundaries, communicating your needs better, and taking the necessary steps to put yourself first rather than always putting others first. It is also a good idea to let the person you share a relationship with understanding what you are going through, how it has affected you and your relationship with them, and what you are going to do to help improve the relationship itself.

As you work toward improving your relationships and engaging in healthier relationship dynamics with people, one of three things is going to happen in each relationship. The person is either going to agree and be supportive, agree after some resistance or disagree or remain resistant to the changes altogether.

When the person agrees and is supportive, you can feel confident that this is going to be a relationship that will be able to foster a healthier dynamic. Chances are, this is someone you can maintain a relationship with for a long time and they will go on to be wonderfully supportive and helpful of all of the changes you are going through. They may also be great people to confide in during your healing journey, depending on who they are and how your relationship with them looks.

When the person agrees with resistance, this could mean a few things. They may be someone who has a hard time changing in general and who genuinely require a few reminders to fully change their behaviors and stop treating you poorly. Or, they may be reluctant to change because the relationship's current dynamics are in some way serving them. Lastly, they might resist the change altogether despite seeming to agree with the need for change because they are benefitting from taking advantage of you and your coping methods. In both of the latter scenarios, you want to seriously consider the future of your relationship with this person as they are unlikely to be healthy for you to keep around. It may be ideal to minimize your contact with them or end the relationship altogether if they never truly change. Remember, no matter how they have treated you in the past, or how you have let them treat you, it is not your obligation to let them continue to treat you poorly now. You have a right to change your mind, require better treatment, and expect change. If they do not change, it is a sign that they do not respect you, even if they claim they do or that they are trying to change. Simply put, someone who wants and cares about change will change, especially if they learn that their existing behaviors are hurting you.

If you come across someone who is completely resistant and refuses your requests or refuses to admit that change is necessary, there is a chance that this is someone abusive. They are likely gaining some form of benefit from you allowing yourself to remain the victim and letting them take advantage of you, and they are completely unwilling to change their behaviors. This is not a person to keep in your circle, no matter who they are because they can be toxic and damaging to you and your self-esteem. Keeping them in your life can impact your ability to move forward and heal, which will directly oppose what you are trying to accomplish. As hard as it might be, you need to let them go and move on in your life.

Build A Healthier Social Circle

Assessing and restructuring your existing circle can be a challenge. For me, doing this resulted in me losing many of my friends and even close relationships with my family because they were simply unwilling to treat me with greater respect, and I was unwilling to accept disrespectful treatment any longer. Part of me staying firm in my boundaries meant ending these relationships and moving on with my life.

It might feel like if you terminate your relationships you are going to be completely alone, especially if this is something your mother has lead you to believe would be true. After all, forcing you to believe that being trapped was the only way to be loved is how she kept you in her cycle of abuse for so long. Understand, however, that there is an entirely different perspective that you can take around this circumstance that might help the process be easier for you.

Understand that terminating relationship and upholding your boundaries does not mean that you are going to be alone. It is not a sign that you are lacking in love, support, compassion, or attention from people in your life. If you let go of these unhealthy relationships, you are not going to be completely forgotten about and abandoned by the world, even if it truly feels that way in your heart. You are not going to be any worse off than you are right now. You are going to be *better* off.

This is not just because you will no longer be exposed to their abuse, even though that is a big part of it. However, an even bigger part is that when you are not wasting all of your energy running in circles and trying to pick yourself up from people's abuse, you have more energy to build healthier relationships in your life. You can focus on meeting new people, people that are completely removed from the abusive part of your life. You can spend time with people who share your interests, and who respect you, and who genuinely enjoy your company and are willing to build a healthy relationship with you. In this, you can even start to explore who you truly are without the influence of abuse when you connect with people who have never known you as a victim.

Building your social circle to include new healthy relationships can help you feel as though you are firmly leaving your past in the past and moving forward. This is a big step in taking control over how you feel, and who you are and reshaping your life without the abuse of others.

As you do build your social circle, make sure you do it at your own pace. This is another great part of your life to include your therapist in, as he or she can help you build these relationships in a way that is not founded on your lack of self-esteem or self-confidence. Instead, they can help you learn to feel empowered and confident in your relationships so that you can genuinely enjoy positive, healthy relationships with new people. You will find that as you do this, and as your relationships get stronger and stronger, your life will continue to improve significantly and you will have more opportunities to feel "normal".

Chapter 15

PROTECTING YOURSELF FROM ABUSE

The final piece in allowing yourself space and opportunity to heal from the abuse is knowing how to protect yourself from future abuse. During my healing process, I found that I had an incredible fear around developing relationships with new people, only to find that they were abusers, too. Because many abusers can go undiscovered for so long before finally showing their true colors, I was terrified of trusting in and caring about anyone for fear that it would turn out terribly. I was truly so untrusting of everyone around me.

You might find that you feel the same way. It might be hard for you to fully trust people or let people in because you are terrified of being abused again by someone new. The idea of getting to know someone and care about someone only to have them hurt you in this painful way seems too much to bear, yet it also seems inevitable at times. At this point, you are using your past to shape your vision of your future, and it is looking as though you do not know how to truly protect yourself from people who want to hurt you or take advantage of you. That makes complete and perfect sense, and it is also an incredibly normal way to feel when you have been abused.

Learning how to protect yourself means giving yourself, and your inner child, the key that you never had before. This is the armor you needed all along to protect yourself from abuse and prevent yourself from being harmed by other people. A large number of your fears will begin to drop when you realize that you now have access to the knowledge around what this protection is and how it works, and the willingness to use it. When you realize that you can protect yourself, you no longer have to worry about someone else harming you because you will be able to protect yourself and spot unhealthy relationships from a mile away. Your confidence in yourself will grow exponentially, and as it does your trust issues will start to become less powerful and scary to live with.

You must learn to protect yourself not only so that you can build your confidence, but also so that you can avoid future instances of abuse. Abuse, in any form, is scary and traumatizing. As someone who has already been abused you are especially vulnerable to being abused again, and knowing how to protect yourself is your key to minimizing your vulnerability and exposure in this area of your life.

Learn to Identify Red Flags and Respect Them

The first thing you need to do when it comes to protecting yourself is to learn about what red flags are, and how to identify them in relationships. Red flags are any sign that indicates a relationship is not ideal for you to be in, and they are always true indicators of what you can expect in the future. When you see a red flag arise in any relationship you are a part of, it is a sign to stop pursuing that relationship. You should always, *always* respect red flags because they never lie.

Some common signs of red flags in relationships include an unwillingness to respect you, overstepping your boundaries even when you have asserted yourself, lying, talking badly about you to your face or others, or ignoring you. Another red flag you should look for, especially with narcissism, is excessive affection early on which can indicate that they are attempting to "love bomb" you – something commonly done by narcissists. When they love bomb, they are trying to show you that they are a perfect match for you, and then they will quietly work on tearing you down through a constant tug-of-war between showing excessive amounts of love and then abusing you. Not all signs of affection or admiration are love bombing, but excessive ones that seem too good to be true might be.

If you notice someone seems to be using you or trying to change you to fulfill their needs, this is also a red flag. People should respect you as you are and not be trying to change you if they do respect you. As well, if they make you feel inadequate, try to come in between you and the things or people you love, or otherwise, try to isolate you, this is a red flag. There are many additional red flags you can look for, depending on what type of relationship you are considering. A great way to identify what you should be looking for, and what it will look like in real life, is through Googling red flags relating to the relationship in question. This way, you can get a deeper understanding of what you are looking for and how to identify it.

Reinforce Your Independence

Another thing you need to do to start protecting yourself is to reinforce your independence.

Continually work on building up your self-confidence, self-esteem, and self-worth through fostering healthier relationships with yourself and with others. The more you can increase your sense of self and your independence, the more you will be able to rely on yourself and trust in yourself. This way, you are less likely to leave yourself exposed to the abuse of anyone in the future.

A great way to continue to reinforce your independence is to get to know yourself better and to have private things, just for you. For example, if you love working out you can make it your private thing to work out regularly. Perhaps for this, you go by yourself and you refuse to invite anyone or cancel your workouts for anyone. Continue doing the things that you do for yourself even when you are in relationships with people, and avoid anyone unwilling to respect your time. Reinforcing your independence both inside and outside of relationships will help you stay stronger in your sense of self, while also minimizing your vulnerability to abuse.

When you do find yourself being exposed to some form of abuse, rely on your independence to help you walk away. Do not be afraid to face the feelings of being alone or abandoned, as you ultimately know this is not true and this will not happen. Reinforce your trust in yourself that you will be safe, loved, and supported no matter what decision you make, and always make the decision that supports your mental, emotional, and physical health.

Have A Plan for What You Will Do?

It is always important to have a plan in place for what you are going to do if you find yourself in an abusive situation, or in a situation where you may be in the process of building a relationship with someone that you realize is abusive. This can happen, especially early on in your recovery, and it can be scary to realize that you are in this situation. Sometimes it can take a while for you to catch on, so the situation may have time to escalate before you understand what is happening.

Even if you feel confident that this will not happen, you should have a plan for what you are going to do to escape that situation. Maintain your independence and use your independence to help you remove yourself from the relationship. For example, have a separate set of friends or loved ones you can rely on for support, stay financially independent, and decide how you are going to walk away. Make a plan for how you will assert your boundaries, how you will avoid further contact with this person, and how you will deal with the painful feelings that come up around this.

Having a plan in place helps you feel safer in knowing that if you ever did find yourself in need, you have a clear way to protect yourself and you are not going to be left alone, confused, and trapped again. This is not your childhood and this person is not your guardian: you do have the right to say no and terminate any relationship for any reason, including one relating to abuse or toxic behaviors. That includes your relationship with your mother if you ever find yourself in the abuse cycle again and in need of an escape plan.

CONCLUSION

I want to take a moment to deeply congratulate you on your willingness to see the truth of your experiences and work toward healing from your narcissistic mother's abuse. Being the daughter of a narcissistic mother is not easy, and recovering from her abuse is not, either. Your decision to put yourself first and take your recovery, and life, into your own hands in this way is a major step in a positive direction and I want you to know that this step is worthy of your celebration.

You are a strong woman, despite how your mother treated you in your childhood. You are not a victim, you are a warrior who is choosing a new path for herself and who is bravely taking action on walking that path, no matter how hard it might be. That is incredible.

Right now, you might be feeling many things. You might be feeling excited to know that there is a future without abuse available to you, or you might be feeling terrified that this is all going to fall apart. Maybe you think it's too good to be true. In either case, I want you to honor how you feel because that is an important part of moving forward.

When I first took big, bold action toward recovering, I went through many different emotions that lead to me feeling like I was going crazy. I would constantly be overcome with huge feelings of relief and excitement, and massive periods of grief and misery. This is all a natural part of the grieving and healing process.

Now, years later, I can honestly say that I have come a long way from the abusive cycles I used to be trapped in with my mother. She no longer has the power to hurt me, and the words that used to ring through my head like knives cutting me down no longer exist. When I do find myself thinking critically about myself in ways that my mother would have when I was younger, I know that this is a form of intrusive thought and I release the thought and forgive myself for letting it come through. Then, I validate myself and move forward.

One day, maybe soon, you too are going to find that your mother no longer has that power over you. You will no longer feel a constant need to try and please her, and the dreaded fear that comes with realizing that you are trapped in this cycle of abuse. You will feel liberated, confident, and *normal*. I cannot say when for sure, but I can say with confidence that if you keep working toward your recovery, you can heal from your mother's abuse.

Please stay consistent in your path and continue working toward your recovery every day, as it will take time for you to fully recover. Be patient with yourself, have compassion for yourself, and show yourself as much love as you can. Trust that you are doing your best in every moment and that your life will get better. You have the power to make that happen, and you are tapping into that power, now.

As you continue to move forward with your healing, be sure to continue educating yourself around what to expect, and surround yourself with people who can help you. The more informed you are, and the more supported you feel, the easier it will be for you to truly move beyond your mother's abuse and into your recovery. Keep building up your support system and leaning into them when you need to, and trust that they are there to help you. They care about you, love you, and want to see you succeed. There are genuine, good people in the world, and you can and will find them and surround yourself with them.

I believe in you.

Before you go, I want to ask you one important favor. If you feel that reading *Narcissistic Mother. It's Not Your Fault.* has helped you in recovering from your mother's narcissism, please take the time to honestly review it on Amazon Kindle. I want to get this book in front of as many people as I possibly can so that I can help more women just like you recover from their abusive situations.

Thank you, and best of luck. You are doing great, and you are never alone.

Printed in Great Britain
by Amazon